HOW TO START YOUR OWN LAW PRACTICE......AND SURVIVE (The summarized quick guide for new lawyers).

By Arvand Naderi, Esq.

INTRODUCTION

I think back to my law school days. I remember that things were so different when I was in school. The pressures are different, the surroundings are different, and the tone of life is different. That is why I decided to write this little piece. I think if newer lawyers are given a set of ideas and rules to at least consider, they can make the first few years' survival rate increase significantly. I know it was scary as hell starting my own practice. It gets easier, and more fruitful as time goes by. I am merely hoping that some of the mistakes I made can be prevented or I can at least make you aware of what is out there.

Throughout this writing, I will relate my own experiences to you. That is the best I can do because it makes sense. I am not just someone who is talking out of his ass, I have been there, actually I am still there, and I am still doing it.

This little thing I wrote will not make you an overnight legal scholar or entrepreneurial genius, but I hope that it will at least make you feel a bit at ease about what goes on in the legal world and in your new practice.

I hope I can help you avoid the mistakes I made and the pitfalls that hindered my practice. Best of luck to you in your endeavors!

DIFFERENT STATES

I passed the bar in California. I know that not everyone reading this is a California attorney. Not to worry. This guide is meant for ALL new attorneys. It is not necessarily state-specific.

KNOW THE LAW

You do not sell a tangible item or product. You get paid for your thoughts and knowledge. So familiarize yourself with your product. Your product is the law. KNOW THE LAW. Every practice area has a practice guide. Probably cost you a couple of hundred dollars. Well worth it. Buy it, and read it. Don't buy it to add to your bookshelf of books you never read. Buy it and read it. Your knowledge of the law is what will impress potential clients. Your ability to answer their questions, your ability to describe procedure. So know the law.

<u>YOUR IMAGE</u>

In a commercial a few years back, Andre Agassi stated that "Image is everything". Well, I am here to tell you that that statement is completely true. When I started out my practice, my office was a dingy hole in the wall. I cannot tell you how important it is to have a nice office. I had lost numerous clients to the appearance of the dingy office in a not-so-great neighborhood. When someone is handing you a check for several thousand dollars, they want to make sure that they are in good hands. If your office appears not so pretty, they will start questioning things. That is a downward spiral you want to avoid. Here is the real-life rule: Potential clients don't care about paying you the big bucks if they see that you deserve it. It is sad but true. Even though you may be an attorney that will bust your ass for your client, they are attracted to the attorney that might not bust his ass for the client....but sits on the 20th floor of a high-powered building with a nice view. You can have the dingier office later on in your practice when you are well-established.

4

The problem is that as a fresh attorney, your funds are most likely limited. That is understandable. There are a couple of ways around this. One, meet with clients at another attorney's office. You will have to pay the attorney to use his office but it is well worth it. Second, meet the client at a coffee shop. The only issue there is that some clients might have an issue with talking to you in a crowded coffee shop. I agree with them on that one so you have to balance it properly. Third, you can offer to meet the client at their residence. This has worked for me before. The only issue is that clients might have numerous family members around who will want to pick your brain for hours about why their landlord does this and that and why they want to terminate their cell phone contract.

Keep in mind that if you go to a client's house, they will see your car. Another "gauge" of how good an attorney you are according to the average person's way of thinking. So if you don't have a nice luxury car, borrow one to take to client meetings.

You should have nice suits and all the nice little accessories like cufflinks and a nice watch. And of course, nice shoes. In the beginning this will be difficult, but do your best. Don't wear old ugly suits. If you have to, charge a few hundred dollars on a credit card and buy yourself a couple of nice, professional suits. I like the Men's Warehouse, or 3-Day suit broker in the valley.

Most people do not realize that an attorney does not know everything there is to know about every type of law. That is ridiculous. When I first started out, I would try to look up every type of question on different types of law. You CANNOT do this without going crazy. So don't do it. The correct response is "I'm sorry, I only practice criminal law....or property law...or family law". Don't get stuck in the never-ending debate with a client. If it is in your field, then answer the question. If you don't know it, then let the client know that you have to look up that answer for him or her. If you don't practice it, then don't practice it.

THE MENTOR

This is a must have in order to survive. Think about this: You are competing with a bunch of attorneys that have been around longer, seen more, and know more. They are not necessarily smarter, they just have more time in the bunker.

You have to find a mentor. There are seasoned attorneys out there that are willing to help you out in your practice. They truly enjoy sharing the gift of knowledge. My suggestion is to join all the groups you can. This includes all bar association groups, and any other groups that consist of attorneys and judges. Once you are in these groups, you let people know that you are just starting out.

My mentor, who is now my partner, was doing a jail visit when I met him. I asked him a simple question about filling out a visitor form and it all started from there. You never know who will turn out to be your mentor but you MUST have one.

Be wary of any mentor that penetrates their concentration on money and nothing else. Before I met my current partner, I tried to establish myself with a couple of other attorneys. Every other sentence would have to do with how much of the retainer they were getting and when the payment will arrive. Bad sign. Run.

You will most likely get a positive response along with a lot of "Here's my card, call me anytime for help". Use that card and make that call. Make sure you follow the business day rule. It goes something like this- most attorneys are stressed and frustrated during the business day, myself included, try to call on Fridays or even leave a message with the service on the weekends. In that message, make sure you let the attorney know that they should contact you at their convenience, not yours. When you do get a call back, you should offer to take the attorney out for lunch or dinner....and actually do it. Once you get your lunch or dinner with the attorney, pick their brain as much as you can. Try to concentrate on procedural questions. What you are really asking the attorney is "How can I not look stupid in court?". They have the answer.

When you are asking questions of a more experience attorney, try to visualize yourself in court, and try to carry out the proceedings in your head and correlate the proceedings to the questions you are asking. Here are some typical questions you should be asking:

1. What happens when I go to court on this type of case or issue?

2. Do I check in first with the clerk?

3. Do I call out my case or does the clerk just put the case up?

4. What is the proper way to start the case out?

5. What questions might the judge ask me?

6. What do I say or do with opposing counsel or the prosecutor?

7. What types of statutory or procedural issues am I facing?

All of the above questions have one goal, and that is to bring your competence level to an aesthetically pleasing foundation. Or in simpler terms, to prevent you from looking stupid...which I still look all the time. It is normal. It is part of the learning process. Remember everyone has been there. There is not one attorney out there that was born with 2, 5, 10, or 30 years of experience.

My first arraignment was an absolute nightmare. I was sworn in on a Friday and had a felony arraignment on the Monday following. I had no clue what the hell was going on. I didn't even know what to say. That would make sense. I had never done it before. When I arrived in court, my stomach was twisting and turning. I pulled through though. The first step, the most important step........leads me to the following section:

THE JUDGES, CLERKS, AND STAFF

My first experience with a court clerk was in criminal court. She took one look at me and immediately knew what was going on. I walked up to her and told her "This is my first court appearance.....What do I say?". I think she thought I was kidding at first. I clarified "No really, this is my first ever court appearance, what do I say....PLEASE HELP ME". She was extremely helpful. She told me everything I needed to say. She helped me through that appearance and still helps me to this day. We have become friends and I will never forget the fact that she came through and helped me out.

You have to treat the court clerks with the utmost absolute respect and courtesy. They hold the key to all that is essential in a court proceeding. Most of them are wonderful people and will help you out with whatever it is you need help with. They day you are disrespectful to a court clerk is the day you will live to regret for years to come. Remember this, your clients will come and go, but the people that work the court system will be around you for years and at times decades.

What do you do when you come across a clerk that is an absolute jerk? Remind yourself that your are in their house, not yours. DO NOT piss off the clerks. They can make your life very difficult. Do not be pompous or arrogant towards them. Treat them the way you would like to be treated.

As far as the judges go, there are good ones and bad ones, mean ones and nice ones, it depends on what court you are in. Whenever you enter a new court, always talk to the bailiff or the clerk. The bailiff and clerk are familiar with the judges they work for. Ask them if there are any special rules that the judge follows. Ask them about any special procedural issues the judge addresses. Ask them if they judge wants you to stand in any particular spot. This all helps you to be more prepared when the judge comes out. Not only will this small amount of research help you look like you belong, but it will also impress the judge. Remember, you are in the judge's house, not the other way around. And of course, don't' be late. Most judges don't start off right at 8:30, and the ones that do expect you there when the doors open. So until you are familiar with a particular judge, be there on time.

If there is no way you are going to be on time, or you have another court appearance to make, call in the matter right away. When I have multiple court appearances in one day, I begin calling courts at 8:20. The conversation should go something like this:

Clerk: Good morning. Department 1.

You: Good morning mam/sir, private counsel calling in the Smith matter

Clerk: When will you be here?

You: About 9:15. I am in Department 2 Downtown. I have a quick arraignment and will head over right away afterwards. May I leave my cell phone number with you mam/sir?

Clerk: Thank you counsel. See you then.

When the judge comes out, he/she will ask the clerk if any counsel have called in on any cases. You want to make sure the judge know you were considerate enough to the court and the court staff to call the case in.

If you are particularly nervous about making an appearance in court, go to that particular court the day or week before and sit down and observe the logistics of that court. That way you can picture yourself making the appearance down the line.

YOUR OFF DAYS

In the beginning of your law practice, you will have a lot of free time on your hands. What do you do with it?

1. Buy a practice guide and read it religiously- For criminal law, it is the CEB guide to California Criminal Law. This guide replaced my usual nightly readings of adult publications. I go to bed with this guide and read chapters here and there. It does not give you real life experience but what it does is give you the tools you need to know the real life experience when it hits. You will see something in court and it will click in your mind. For other practice areas, there are how to guides as well. BUY THEM! READ THEM!

2. Go to court- Put your suit on, go and sit in court, and listen and pay attention. This is a great habit because you pick up the key phrases and nuances that will make you look and feel like you know what you are talking about...even if you don't. If you are going to practice landlord-tenant law, go and watch eviction proceedings. If you are going to practice criminal law, go and watch preliminary hearings. You will be amazed at the amount of knowledge you will pick up just by going to court. More importantly, your face will become familiar in the court system.

3. Court cafeteria- One of the more important areas in your life as an attorney. Everyone passes through the court café. Judges, attorneys, bailiffs, and clerks all have to drink coffee and eat sometime. This is where it all happens. Get your face in there, grab a cup of coffee, and smile and say hello to people that pass you by as you sit in the café. Recognize who the judges are and what departments they are in. Learn to associate the bailiffs and other court staff with their assigned departments.

<u>ADVERTISING</u>

You have to be very selective and careful with your advertising. Advertising overhead can add up quicker than a crackheads convictions. When you are just starting out, you have to be frugal with your dollars.

Yellow Pages- Initially I placed a business card sized ad in the yellow pages. I had enough calls and cases to make up for the costs. Later on, I took out 8 whole pages in the yellow pages and had horrendous results. I was getting more calls from my smaller ads than from the full page ads. My advice here- contrary to what you may have heard, smaller is better......at least with yellow page advertising.

T.V. Ads- Too expensive when you are starting out. Something to look into down the line. The problem with T.V. ads is that it takes a while for the ads to work. Your name is basically what you are trying to sell on T.V. You want it to get to a point that people associate your name with the type of law you are practicing. That takes months of repetitive T.V. advertising which equates to tons of dollars before you ever see any returns. Don't get me wrong, you will get calls quickly, but the problem is that your call retainers have to equal more than your expenses. I would stay away initially.

Networking groups- A great and inexpensive way to get your business card out. Highly recommended. Go to local city networking clubs, they all have them and they love new members.

Website- Extremely important. Create a website as soon as possible. You probably do not have much to post when you first start out so post general information such as client rights, the legal procedure and system, and other basic information. For my website, www.wehatejail.com, http://www.idefendyou.org, I use Ontrix Solutions, located in West Hills, California. They also do a program for me where a potential client enters information such as "criminal lawyer Los Angeles", and somewhere in the results is my website. This is called Search Engine Optimization. A great way to attract clients. SEO however, can become costly. As of now though, it is the big thing in advertising for attorneys. There are two types, the pay per click, where you pay whenever someone clicks on your ads, usually highlighted on the top of right of the page, and the natural or organic, where your name is in the results down the middle of the page. This is great advertising but obviously the stronger the keywords (the more the other lawyers are willing to pay for them), the more expensive the advertising will cost you.

Another important portion of your website should be something like a testimonials, of previous client statement page. You have to have this. After I finish every case, I ask my clients to fill out a testimonial page. I assure them that I will only use their initials when referring to the testimonial. I place most of the testimonials of my webpage. It has gotten to a point now that I have a bunch on there and am not worried about updating it as much. I will update it once a year or so and add the new testimonials.

Testimonials are important as they will serve as a pivot point for potential clients. In other words, a new client may be considering retaining you, but they are not sure. You tell them, feel free to check out my site and what some of my previous clients have said about me. They may check out the site, they may not. If they do, they would read something positive that a former client has said about you. This would be the key in closing a new client. You are a good attorney, you will fight hard for your client, but you can tell them this all day and it won't mean crap. It will mean a lot though, when coming from someone that has been where the potential new client is going.

17

Another form of advertising is the referral letter. Sit down and write a letter to other attorneys, and simply ask them for business. Something like this:

Dear Attorney A,

Please allow me to take a moment to introduce myself....my name is new lawyer B and I practice exclusively personal injury law, or criminal law, (or whatever you practice).

I am writing this letter with the hopes that we may have complementary practices. (Talk a little more about what it is you do).......then get to the most important part.

I offer a __% referral fee to attorneys for their referrals. This fee is paid in accordance with the State Bar guidelines.

Send out a letter like that to every attorney you know that DOES NOT practice in your particular field. Sit down and go through the Yellow Pages, or do online searches to find other attorneys. I have gotten a good amount of business using this method.

Another step that might help is to include something unique such as a magnet, pen, or small calendar with your business name on it. That way your letter does not make it straight into the trash. Your item will be held on to and your name and the type of law you practice will be associated with that item, whether it be a pen or calendar.

The best advertising- WORD OF MOUTH. Almost all of my big cases have come from referrals. That is why it is so important to get out there and get your business cards out to everyone that you can.

Finally, go to where your potential clients are. If you practice criminal defense, you want criminals. If you practice wills and trusts, you want older people. If you practice family law, you want unhappily married people. Find out where your potential clients are located, and be visible.

Family- After you pass the bar and start your practice, make sure you let your family members know they type of law you are practicing. They are not psychic and are probably under the impression (as are most laypeople), that you are all-seeing and all-powerful in all areas of law. Clear that up for them. Let them know that when someone gets arrested, to call you, or if someone wants a divorce, to call you. Give your family members business cards.

BUSINESS CARDS

Your key to survival. A great place to order business cards is www.gotprint.com. They have a 5000 business card special for $99 or so. I don't know if they still have it but it is worth looking. The cards are high quality and my favorite. I have gotten more compliments on their cards than on the more expensive "American Psycho" type of cards. For letterhead, I use www.vistaprint.com. They have the special letterhead you can make, add a legal logo to make it pretty, and they also have the continuation sheets. You get a total of about 500 total sheets for a hundred fifty dollars or so. Not a bad deal.

Your business cards are your way of making a living. Carry a stack of them on you at ALL times. Always have a card ready to give out at stores, other businesses, meetings, bars, court and bathrooms. The last one is optional.

I make it a habit to hand out a card to a new person everyday. Think about it this way, you are providing a valuable service for a living. Why not let people

20

know about it? When I meet someone new, I ask about them and what they do and at the end of the conversation I say by the way, here's my card, if I can be of any assistance, please let me know. That simple.

You just don't know when a new person will turn into a future client. I gave a recent client of mine a business card almost a year before he became my client. Calls me up out of the blue, says he got arrested, and I signed him up as a new client. Always give out your business card. Make a plan to give out a certain number of cards everyday. The goal is to have your card in the hands of as many people as possible. Everyday give out 5, or 10, or 2. Just give them out. It is like an investment. It will come back to payoff in the future sometime, you just don't know when.

AN ACCOUNTANT AND TAXES

Just like you have to have a good lawyer, you have to have a good accountant. Find someone that is reasonable, ethical, and someone that gets the work done on time. My C.P.A. is a guy name Ray Hebrank (818) 712-9550, he is located in Canoga Park. I am very happy with him. Gets the work done, advises me on what to do......as I am absolutely clueless on anything having to do with taxes.

When it comes to having your own business, you have to hang on to your receipts. Everything that you do in the name of the business should be evidenced by a receipt and that receipt should be held on to. I do it this way, whatever I buy or spend money on for the business I get a receipt for, I put all the receipts together every month and mail them off to my C.P.A. He keeps track of it all for me. You have to pay for this obviously, but it's worth it. You need to have a professional keep track of all your business stuff. By a professional, I don't mean you the lawyer, I mean a C.P.A. trained to deal with income, taxes, and other related issues.

Ray also told me to incorporate. You can have the articles of incorporation done for a few hundred dollars and you are good to go. Apparently, and quote me on this, as again, I am clueless with any and all tax and business items, there are benefits to incorporating, such as tax benefits and corporate protection.

When you are initially finding a C.P.A., be honest with him/her. Let them know you are just starting out and you don't have unlimited resources. You are looking for a C.P.A. to grow with you. Ask them if they are willing to be that C.P.A. If they are, then give it a shot.

Remember, especially if you are self-employed, your finances are going to get more and more complicated. That is why you need a professional, preferably one that has been there from day one, to guide you through the mess.

ETHICS

I learned when I first started out my practice that your name is the most important thing you have in this game. Everything rides on your name. Every client that you come in contact with will come and go. Their cases, their facts, their dilemmas, will all come and go. Your reputation will not. It will remain with you FOREVER. Do not tarnish it. Do not jeopardize it. Do not sell yourself out.

What do I mean by that? Well, some clients will ask you to do things that may seem borderline. Others will ask you to do things that are outright unethical, outrageous, and deadly to your career. You worked hard for your ticket, and your ticket should not be put on the line for anything or any amount. Always be ethical.

I will give an example. A couple years back one of my clients friends came to my office with a brand new Rolex. A beautiful watch. They wanted to pay the retainer with the watch. I thanked them for their time, and told them that the risk of that watch being stolen was not worth risking my bar card. That simple. No hesitation on my part. They told me that other lawyers have taken property from them before. I told them to go to the other lawyers.

In the end, I lost money on that case. I was not paid my entire retainer. And that was fine. I could sleep at night. And you can't put a price tag on that.

You should not only be cautious about situations like that, but the alarms in your head should be going off anytime something like that comes up.

As far as ethics go, every state has their set of rules and laws. Here, with the California Bar, California Attorneys can call up a number and anonymously ask questions that they do not know the answers to. I recommend that. If you don't know....ASK. Better safe that sorry. If something does not sound right...ASK. Don't ever feel guilty, or ashamed, or intimidated. Always, ask yourself whether your bar card is worth it. The answer is always no.

MALPRACTICE INSURANCE

I did a lot of research when it came to finding the best rates on malpractice insurance. The company that had the best rates, based on my research of California companies, was Lawyers Mutual Insurance Company. They are located in Burbank, CA. They have special programs for attorneys just starting out in their first, second, and other years of practice. I find the staff to be helpful and knowledgeable. For the out of staters, you can do a simple search in Google. Call at least 5 malpractice insurance companies before choosing one.

I would recommend maintaining malpractice insurance. It is a good idea to protect yourself.

IN THE END

Beginning the practice of law can be extremely challenging. There are many pitfalls and obstacles. I hope that this little guide can give you some ideas on what to do, what to avoid, and how to conduct yourself. Here are some general ideas to keep in mind:

1. Know the law- Read the practice guides, talk to more experienced attorneys.

2. In the beginning, keep your expenses low. Use as many free resources as you can.

3. Always network. Make it a point to meet someone new everyday. Tell them about what you do and give them a business card. Make it a rule to give out 1-3 business cards a day.

4. ALWAYS be ethical. There is no client worth your bar card. There is no dollar amount that can be put on the blood and sweat that you put into obtaining your bar card.

5. Email me if you need help. Wehatejail@hotmail.com

I wish you the best in your future endeavors and the beginning of your law practice.